Emotional Intelligence

Top 20 Daily Tips to Master Your Emotions, Increase Your EQ, Improve Interpersonal Skills, and Become More Emotionally Intelligent in All Aspects of Life!

Contents

Introduction

I want to thank and congratulate you for downloading *"Emotional Intelligence: Top 20 Daily Tips to Master Your Emotions, Increase EQ, Improve Interpersonal Skills, and Become More Emotionally Intelligent in All Aspects of Life."*

Having high IQ is one thing—but what about EQ?

In life, it is not only important to be smart and well-read. You also have to make sure that you're emotionally intelligent, too. You see, you won't be able to relate to others if you're like a robot that just repeats and does what people tell him to.

In order to be a successful person, you have to make sure that you also know how to put yourself in others' shoes, and that while you begin to be sensitive—in a good way—you also would not let your emotions get the best of you.

With the help of this book, you'd learn how to be in control of your emotions, and develop high EQ—or Emotional Quotient—to become a whole, well-mannered, and successful person in all aspects of your life!

Read on and find out how!

Once again, thank you and good luck!

Chapter 1: Master Your Emotions

Before anything else, you have to learn how to master your emotions. You have to understand that you're in this world not to let your emotions rule your life, but to have some power over them.

Once you do this, you'll be able to mingle with people more, and you would no longer let your emotions stop you from being the person you're meant to be! Here's how:

1. Managing Hurt

More than anything, hurt could be detrimental to your life because when you're in pain, you get to feel like there's nothing you can do to make your life better.

This is wrong. No matter how hurt or heartbroken you are, you can still take control of your life. Here are a few simple steps you could follow.

a) **Communicate the hurt.** You can either talk to the person who hurt you, or someone you trust. Let things out and air your side.

b) **If number 1 is not possible, get a piece of paper or a journal and write about how you feel.** Exorcise your demons.

c) **Sometimes, expectations cause hurt.** Make a list of your expectations, read them again, and check if they are actually doable or if they're too much. Remind yourself that everyone is a human—you cannot expect something that you yourself are not willing to give.

d) **Try to look at your life from afar.** Ask yourself how

you feel, and what makes you feel bad. Then, try to see if you could weed out some toxic people or situations in life.

Remember: While you do not always know what's going to happen next, you can take control of the hurt. You can choose to be happy—and there is nothing wrong with that.

2. Managing Fear and Discomfort

Fears are scary because they can lead to discomfort. They can lead you to think that you can't do something just because you are scared of it. They'll make you feel uncomfortable, but you know what? More often than not, it's just all in the mind. Try the exercise below and you'll be able to say goodbye to fear and discomfort for good!

a) **Make a list of your fears.**

b) **Choose one of those fears that you can focus on at the moment,** and then sit straight or lie down on your back. Close your eyes—but make sure that you wouldn't sleep.

c) **Hold one part of your body** (i.e., the toes, the knees), breathe deeply, and say: *I welcome resistance and infuse it with love and light.* Repeat until you feel relaxed.

d) **Talk to the fear.** Talk about why it's there, and why it became your fear in the first place. Thank him

e) **Finally, talk to the fear again.** Say goodbye. Say you're ready to take charge of your life now. This way, you can finally heal and let go.

3. Managing Anger

Next, it is important for you to manage anger so that you wouldn't let it cloud your decisions. Remember that anger doesn't often lead to the best decisions, so you have to manage it head on. Here's how:

a) **Try to understand why you're angry—and then see how you can let the anger out.** Scream, write, talk to the person you're angry at, etc.

b) **Reevaluate your rules in life.** Are people really making you angry? Or, maybe, it's you who's making yourself angry because you have unrealistic expectations? Learn to understand that your life is different from everybody else's—so do not try to put up the same rules as others.

c) **Rules do not have to be applied in every circumstance.** Remember that each event that happens in your life is different from the rest, so do not be someone who feels the need to make use of the same rules for different situations in life. That just won't work.

d) **Do not deny your anger**—but don't let it control you, either. Recognize why you're angry, but don't let it rule over your life.

e) **Let go.** Once you have aired your anger, and once you know you have done something to recognize it, learn to let go. You don't have to let this anger make decisions for you every day of your life.

4. Managing Inadequacy and Frustration

Next, it's time to manage frustration and inadequacy.

No one is perfect—and that's why in life, you'd often feel frustrated or inadequate especially when you feel like you have not done enough. But oftentimes, it's not that you haven't done enough—it's more like you're just not used to adept to this certain thing, and you know what? That's okay.

Listed below are ways to help you manage inadequacy and frustration:

a) **Make a list of your strengths**. Remind yourself of what you're good at and you'd realize that while you're not perfect, you're not actually that bad either. There is always something you're good at—keep that in mind.

b) **Think outside the box.** Maybe, you're not getting the results you want because you're thinking the same way as others. You don't have to do that. Remember that you can always create your own path and make your own ways.

c) **Try to review what you have done before**. What were the mistakes you made in the past that you no longer want to repeat? How can you manage not to repeat them? By thinking back on what you've done, you'll get some clarity about what you're supposed to do.

d) **Remember that you are enough**. Don't push yourself too hard, but don't slack off, either. Just do your best!

5. Managing Loneliness and Disappointment

And finally, you have to let go of disappointment and loneliness. Unless you're diagnosed with Depression and the like, you have to realize that you have the power to control your mind and your emotions. Here's how you can let go of loneliness and disappointment:

a) **Remember that you are disappointed because you have feelings**. That's okay. While things may not have gone your way today, just think about the fact that they can be better tomorrow. Every day is different!

b) **Think about what you really want to do in life**. Sometimes, you only get disappointed because of goals that you have not made come true yet. Break your goals down into smaller ones, and see what you can do each day that would benefit you in the long run.

c) **Make an effort.** Maybe, you're lonely because you feel alone and you aren't making progress in life. Well, make an effort to put yourself out there. Talk to people. Write your mission and vision in life. Get to know yourself better. Help someone in need.

There are so many things that you can do to make yourself feel like you're a part of this world. Focus on that, and stop thinking you are alone. You are not.

Chapter 2: How to Increase EQ

Now, it's time for you to improve your Emotional Quotient, also known as EQ. When you have high EQ, you become more aware of what's going on around you, and you also develop better relationships with the people in your life. You also tend to understand things better, as well!

Here are ways that would help you increase EQ!

6. Learning to be Self-Aware

First, you have to learn how to be self-aware. Self-awareness is said to be the root of all strong characters because it helps you understand and accept your successes and failures.

In order to be more self-aware, here's what you should know:

a) **Write your plans and priorities**. You have to decide what matters to you, and stop being just like a "leaf in the wind".

b) **Meditate.** But, it's not just your normal kind of meditation where you sit down and breathe. Instead, you should go ahead and ask yourself the questions given below while sitting in silence:
   What is it that I really am trying to achieve?
   Am I working hard to achieve what I want?
   What slows me down?
   What is it about my life that I need to change?

c) **Get feedback**. Ask your family, friends and workmates what they think of you as a person and as a co-worker. Sometimes, in order to get to know yourself better, you have to see yourself from others' perspectives.

d) **Take psychometric tests**. These tests will help you know what you're doing right and give you answers as to what you're really good at—so you could eventually make a career out of it!

7. Building Empathy

Developing Empathy is important because you get to remind yourself that other people also go through certain things in life, and that as a person, it's good to put yourself in their shoes so you could see life through their eyes.

You see, by being in tune with your emotions, you also learn to understand what others are going through. You do not become prejudiced or judgmental. Instead, you learn how to see where they're coming from—and you begin to realize that people really have different lives to live. Then, they begin to relate to you, and know that you're someone they could trust—and that's exactly what you'd like to happen!

You can build empathy by doing the following:

a) **Be curious about the people you meet.** Do not see them as plain strangers, but rather as people who are also going through things. Remember that each person you see has a story.

b) **Put yourself in other people's shoes.** It is such a cliché, but it works. Once you learn to put yourself in other people's shoes, you also begin to see how their mind works. When people around you make certain decisions that make you raise your eyebrows, understand where they are coming from. Remember they are not you.

c) **Listen—and also learn how to open up**.

d) **Be ambiguous.** Learn to see different sides of any given situation. This doesn't mean you're going to side with the bad people, but rather that you'd also learn to see what made them that way—or why things ended up this way.

8. Learning to Motivate Oneself

If there's one important thing you should remember, it's the fact that it is up to you to motivate yourself.

Sometimes, though, life makes it seem hard for you to appreciate what you have—and help you remind yourself that you should go on. At times like this, just remember these guidelines below:

a) **Pre-commit when you know you're going to procrastinate**. This means that you should remind yourself that you are already committed to something, because with that thought in mind, you could push yourself not to procrastinate.

b) **Know that others are relying on you**. In this world, no man is an island. Whatever it is that you're doing in life is significant to others' lives, too.

c) **Make use of a vision boa**rd. Put it where you'd always see it to remind yourself of where you're going. Add quotes that you know will motivate you.

d) **Create Momentum**. Instead of saying you're going to get $10,000 in a month, think about what you can do each day to get there first. Think about what you can make it a week first. There is nothing wrong with starting small.

e) **Remember that for everything you finish, you get a chance to move on to the next level of success.** This is so much better than getting stuck where you are!

9. Learning to Self-Regulate

Self-Regulation is always deemed to be one of the best behavioral traits that one could have. Self-regulation helps you act in your best interest by making use of your core values.

Basically, this consists of three parts, which are:

a) **Approach**. You have to make a decision as to how you approach things. Will you approach them head-on, or will you wait for a while? Will you be someone who holds his head high, or would you allow others to talk you into doing certain things?

b) **Attack.** Now, you have to decide how you'd attack things. What would help you make things work? How do you think you're supposed to do it? And, when things do not go your way, what would you do? Will you insult or criticize? Would you undermine or dominate? You have to know what your fight response is.

c) **Avoid**. Finally, you have to know what you do not want to deal with in life. As they say, you could choose your battles—it's not like you have to deal with every single thing you encounter all the time.

By being able to self-regulate, it's like you to get to define yourself better. You get to create your "brand", and when this happens, you don't become confused as to how to make decisions and go forth with your life.

10. Basking in Happiness

Finally, in order to raise EQ, you also have to learn how to bask in happiness. Sometimes, people fail to recognize happy moments and they just end up feeling like there's nothing to be happy about.

You see, it's not about chasing happiness: It's more about recognizing it. You have to allow yourself to be happy, or else, you'd just feel like life is a series of nothings—and that's not really how you'd want to feel inside.

Here's what you should learn about basking in happiness:

a) **You can choose to be happy.** You can choose to focus on the good stuff, instead of wallowing in things you cannot fix right away.

b) **Remember that little things are also big things.** Sure, you're not a millionaire yet, but you have enough money to drive you by. Or, what about the fact that the person you like smiled at you, or your boss told you that he believes in you? Those little things are enough to be thankful for—and are enough to make you happy. It's not settling—it's appreciating.

c) **Realize that not everyone has what you have.** Stop looking for what you don't have and start appreciating what you have right now.

d) **Moments are fleeting.** They'll pass by—and sooner or later, you'd regret the fact that you chose to be sad when really, you could've just been happy!

Chapter 3: Improve Interpersonal Skills

Interpersonal Skills are skills that would help you communicate with others every day of your life. In short, they'll be able to build better relationships with people at home or at work. Here are some ways for you to improve the said skills.

11. Improve Verbal Communication Skills

First, of course, are your conversation skills. Some people take things too literally, and that's why you have to make sure that you're able to relay what you want them to understand, instead of making them feel confused.

Here's what you can do:

a) Don't act like you're attacking someone. For example, instead of saying *"Why do you like that politician?"* just say, *"Politics is quite colorful, isn't it?"* and then let the other person open up.

b) Don't feel anxious about ending conversations. Conversations do not have to last forever—that's just impossible!

c) Don't pretend to be someone that you're not. Real wit comes from simply being yourself—not from pretending that you are "witty" and that you're a good conversationalist.

d) Don't start things too heavily. Start by talking about the weather, or with paying the other person a compliment. Or, you can start with an observation (i.e., *Have you seen last night's weather news? I thought it was going to rain today...*). You have to make the other person feel like you're not out to judge—or get him. Never start with religion or politics!

e) Feel free to talk to strangers—especially when they do

not look sketchy.
f) Give compliments!
g) Interact with your coworkers and neighbors.
h) Learn how to open up—and do not expect the other person to open up if you yourself won't. Conversations are always two-way streets!
i) Once you have spoken for a while, and if you're both comfortable, you could move on to more personal topics.
j) Pay attention to the person you're talking to. Do not take up all the "airtime".
k) Setup get-togethers for your family or friends.
l) Show some vulnerability. Remember that it's okay to admit you're nervous. It's okay to self-deprecate a bit—it makes you more genuine, as opposed to just putting yourself on an extremely high pedestal.

12. Improve Non-Verbal Communication Skills

Next, you should also try to develop your non-verbal communication skills. Sometimes, you have to let people read between the lines. To practice, follow the guidelines below:

a) Always lean forward and keep your head up.
b) Ask help from a friend to watch you while you practice so he could also provide you with the comments that you need.
c) Make sure not to cross your arms.
d) Make sure that you try to practice one skill at a time so that you wouldn't be overwhelmed and you would still be natural.
e) Make sure to smile warmly and make appropriate eye contact while talking.

f) Once you're confident enough, try it out in real-life situations.

g) Stand close when talking to others so you could make them feel like you're inviting them to your world, and you have no problem being invited in theirs.

h) Try practicing in front of a mirror. This will help you see what you need to change or improve right away.

i) Watch for your tone of voice. Make it clear and confident—but never arrogant.

13. Have Good Manners

Manners are so important because they give people a reflection of who you are.

Truth is, you won't always get a lot of time to help people get to know you, and that's why the impressions you'll make will definitely make a mark. They'll show people that you have values—and that you're meant to be trusted!

Other benefits of having good manners include:

a) **You gain positive attention**. Instead of people raising their eyebrows, people will give you nods and smiles and might even tell others that you're one to watch out for—in a good way.

b) **Sales/success might increase**. Suppose you're in a store or you're at the office and you get to talk to a lot of people. The way you talk to them has a lot to say about what kind of person you are—and will reflect your company or whatever it is that you're representing, as well. Now, would you want them to think negatively of your brand?

c) **Loyalty will be created**. People would want to be associated with you more because they know you're a good person!

d) **You'd be more confident**. With good manners, you become more confident because you know you're not doing anything wrong—and people would have nothing bad to say!

14. Know How to Listen

Listening is an important interpersonal skill. You see, conversations are not just about one person talking, but about making sure that both of you listen. Here are some ways that would help you improve your listening skills:

a) **Always pay attention.** Don't make the person you're conversing with feel like you'd rather be anywhere but there. It's not like you're going to talk all the time, after all, so give him your time of day.

b) **Show him that you're listening.** Stop tinkering with your phone or looking somewhere else. Would you want others to do that with you, too?

c) **Respond appropriately.** Don't overreact, and do not under-react.

d) **Defer judgment.** Keep your biases outside the door and just focus on this conversation, and not on what happened in the past. You don't have to judge the person you're talking to. Don't treat every conversation as if it's a debate of some sorts.

15. Be Accountable for Your Actions

Lastly, when it comes to improving interpersonal skills, you have to make sure that you accountable for your own actions. This means you wouldn't blame others for whatever's happening in your life—and you'd be a more mature person.

Benefits of accountability include:

a) **A sense of responsibility.** Successful, emotionally intelligent people are responsible people. This isn't just about being responsible in good times, but also realizing that you can be responsible even at times when things don't go your way—and that you don't have to blame anyone else.

b) **You'll be empowered.** There is nothing more empowering than knowing you have the capacity to do a lot of different things in your life. This way, you won't feel like someone else is dictating the course of your life for you. You'd feel like every compliment matters, because you're responsible for your own actions.

c) **You'll be more honest.** A life of honesty is good because you don't get to hide who you really are from others. By being accountable for your actions, you get to show others who you really are—and you don't rely on others to live your life!

Chapter 4: How to be Emotionally Intelligent in All Aspects of Life

Finally, you should also learn how to be emotionally intelligent in all aspects of your life! Here are five simple ways to do so!

16. Manage Your Impulses

An emotionally intelligent person is one who has self-control, and one who knows how to manage his impulses.

There are three types of impulse approaches that you should learn, and these are:

a. **Analytic.** Analytic approaches are all about thinking of the given situation. Some of the questions you should ask yourself include:

> *What makes me think about this certain event?*
>
> *What makes me think of this as a problem?*
>
> *What is an alternative thought that I could replace this with?*

b. **Distractive.** Sometimes, when you see problems or negative situations arise, you could choose to just distract yourself—not to escape from the problem, but to still be able to focus on what you have to do. In short, you'd still get to run towards something, instead of away from something—and you get to control your mind from making you feel like you won't succeed.

c. **Coping.** Finally, you have to make use of coping strategies. These are things you'd tell yourself in order to stop thinking negatively. Some of the things you could tell yourself include:

> *I am in control of my mind; my mind does not control me.*

> *I can think about this.*

> *I am allowed to slow down.*

> *There are always alternatives.*

> *I don't have to rush things.*

Remember: you do not have to give in to your impulses—you are way bigger than them!

17. Be Socially Responsible

You also have to learn to be socially responsible. This means that you are aware that every person has a role in society—and that whatever you do may affect society as a whole.

In order to be socially responsible, you could try the following:

a) **Donate to causes/charities**. Any small amount you have could contribute to a great cause! It will make you feel better, too, because you know you have done something right.

b) **Get involved in charities, marathons, walkathons, pie bakes, and any other cause that you believe in.** It's a good way of being one with people—especially those who think the same way you do.

c) **Be passionate about what you're doing**. Don't do things half-assed—give your best, no matter how small the tasks seem to be. When something is done with love and care, you can expect that they'll yield amazing results.

Remember: It's always good to give back and help others out! Don't be someone who has no care in the world!

18. Control Your Responses

Controlling your responses is a good way of showing others that you understand them, and that you're not just letting your emotions decide for you. A good control of your emotions shows how mature and emotionally intelligent you are.

There are three main aspects that you should look at in order to control your responses. These are:

a) **Event—Define the Event.** An event is not just something big—it could be anything that makes you feel something inside. It could be a comment of your coworker (Your hair looks different today, you have something in your lips, your desk is untidy, etc.), the behavior of your partner (he seems off, his eyes seems crossed, etc.), the weather—anything. Now, what you have to do is think about how you usually react in situations like that. Just think or write about it—for now.

b) **Response—Understanding the Response.** The next thing you have to do is think about your responses for each situation. For example, when the skies turn dark, you often feel scared. When your partner seems off, you just want to argue with him. When your coworker couldn't keep his comments to himself, you tend to feel so bad about yourself.

You see, the thing is that your responses are actually valid. You react to certain things because they tap something inside you. You responses are actually comprised of your thoughts, emotions, and behavior—which is exactly why people react to things in different ways.

For example, if you've had such a rough life, even the littlest things could make you feel so bad about yourself—and make you depressed. But remember, every second that you spend depressed is another second you would not be able to get back. When you let the world win, you're letting yourself lose—is that what you want?

c) **Outcome—The Outcome.** Now, it's time for you to change your response. When your co-worker comments on your hair, thank her about it—and she just might feel like she was burned. You have the choice whether to be affected by someone's comments or not, and you know what? It's best for you to turn it around. When you shape your responses, you shape the outcome of what your life would be. Instead of getting bummed by those comments, you get to feel better about yourself— and work the best way you could!

19. Learn to Accept Your Failures

Then, you also have to learn that you are not perfect—and no one else is, either. By learning to understand that sometimes, you'd make mistakes, you get to help yourself realize that you are human—and you can take things with a grain of salt! This way, you won't get mad or be in pain when you fail—you'd see roadblocks as challenges to success—and not as hindrances.

Here's how you can practice to accept defeat from time to time:

a) **Detach your ego.** Remind yourself that you are just like everyone else, and you are not someone who's always going to be perfect—no matter how much you want to be. Once you learn to get back

28

down to earth, you'll see that life would be so much easier!

b) **Look back at some of your failures—and what happened after them**. For example, you lost the person whom you considered as the love of your life—but what happened after? You rebuilt yourself, right? You got to be successful on your own! With every failure comes success—even those you didn't see coming!

c) **Always think like a scientist**. Why? Well, scientists make a lot of observations and experiments before they get to prove something. Of course, they'd fail. They already know that they will, and yet, they continue doing experiments. This is because they know that sooner or later, they'd be able to get something right—and that hope keeps them going!

20. Cultivate the Attitude of Gratitude

And finally, it's best to be the kind of person who cultivates the attitude of gratitude.

A person who's full of gratitude is someone who knows how to appreciate what he has. Being content does not mean you're not going to do anything to change your life, but is actually a way of letting joy into your life.

According to the Chinese Philosopher Lao Tzu, a person becomes truly rich when he realizes that he actually has enough. This means that each day of your life, its best that you cultivate the attitude of gratitude!

To do so, you can follow the guidelines below:

1. **Keep a gratitude rock**. It could be a piece of marble, a small clean rock—anything that you can keep in your pocket or your purse. The key here is to remember to be thankful for even the smallest things in life—every time you touch the rock! For example, the fact that you woke up this morning, how you got to work early, some spare change—anything!

2. **Keep a gratitude journal**. Write down anything you're thankful for—and make sure to do it each day.

3. **Create your gratitude wheel**. Think of a color wheel, but instead of colors, categorize the wheel depending on who and what you're thankful for in your life!

4. **String a few beads, and think about who and what you're thankful for as you run your fingers on each of the beads.**

See? There are so many things that you can do each day to help yourself be grateful! A grateful person is a master of his emotions—and that's certainly what you'd like to be!

Conclusion

Thank you for reading this book!

Hopefully, this book has opened up your mind about why Emotional Intelligence needs to be developed, and how it could help you out.

Don't forget to apply what you have learned in your daily life. Sooner or later, you'd see how great they'd make you—and the world around you—feel.

Finally, if you enjoyed this book, please take time to post a review on Amazon. It will be greatly appreciated.

Thank you and enjoy!

If you enjoyed this book, maybe you will also enjoy some of our other books:

Easiest Diet Plan that Actually Works and One of the Best Books Hands Down!

http://bit.ly/GreatDiet

Fun and Daring Book Texting Books (18+ Please)

http://bit.ly/HotTexting

Are you In charge of your Emotions or is it the Other Way Around?

http://bit.ly/Emotional EQ

Chess: Strategies and Tactics Book

http://bit.ly/Next_Level_Chess

Dealing with a Break Up Book

http://bit.ly/Heart_Break

Like us on FaceBook:
https://www.facebook.com/Toppickbookpublishing/

And Visit us at: www.toppickink.com

Hope to hear from you soon and Thank You for your Business!

Sincerely,

Top Pick

Made in the USA
San Bernardino, CA
25 March 2017